My Bilingual Picture Book

Mein zweisprachiges Bilderbuch

Sefa's most beautiful children's stories in one volume

Ulrich Renz • Barbara Brinkmann:

Sleep Tight, Little Wolf · Schlaf gut, kleiner Wolf

For ages 2 and up

Cornelia Haas • Ulrich Renz:

My Most Beautiful Dream · Mein allerschönster Traum

For ages 2 and up

Ulrich Renz • Marc Robitzky:

The Wild Swans · Die wilden Schwäne

Based on a fairy tale by Hans Christian Andersen

For ages 5 and up

© 2024 by Sefa Verlag Kirsten Bödeker, Lübeck, Germany. www.sefa-verlag.de

Special thanks to Paul Bödeker, Freiburg, Germany

All rights reserved.

ISBN: 9783756304349

Read · Listen · Understand

Sleep Tight, Little Wolf
Schlaf gut, kleiner Wolf

Ulrich Renz / Barbara Brinkmann

English — bilingual — German

Translation:

Pete Savill (English)

Audiobook and video:

www.sefa-bilingual.com/bonus

Password for free access:

English: `LWEN1423`

German: `LWDE1314`

Good night, Tim! We'll continue searching tomorrow.
Now sleep tight!

Gute Nacht, Tim! Wir suchen morgen weiter.
Jetzt schlaf schön!

It is already dark outside.

Draußen ist es schon dunkel.

What is Tim doing?

Was macht Tim denn da?

He is leaving for the playground.

What is he looking for there?

Er geht raus, zum Spielplatz.

Was sucht er da?

The little wolf!

He can't sleep without it.

Den kleinen Wolf!

Ohne den kann er nicht schlafen.

Who's this coming?

Wer kommt denn da?

Marie! She's looking for her ball.

Marie! Die sucht ihren Ball.

And what is Tobi looking for?

Und was sucht Tobi?

His digger.

Seinen Bagger.

And what is Nala looking for?

Und was sucht Nala?

Her doll.

Ihre Puppe.

Don't the children have to go to bed?
The cat is rather surprised.

Müssen die Kinder nicht ins Bett?
Die Katze wundert sich sehr.

Who's coming now?

Wer kommt denn jetzt?

Tim's mum and dad!

They can't sleep without their Tim.

Die Mama und der Papa von Tim!

Ohne ihren Tim können sie nicht schlafen.

More of them are coming! Marie's dad.
Tobi's grandpa. And Nala's mum.

Und da kommen noch mehr! Der Papa von Marie.
Der Opa von Tobi. Und die Mama von Nala.

Now hurry to bed everyone!

Jetzt aber schnell ins Bett!

Good night, Tim!

Tomorrow we won't have to search any longer.

Gute Nacht, Tim!

Morgen müssen wir nicht mehr suchen.

Sleep tight, little wolf!

Schlaf gut, kleiner Wolf!

Cornelia Haas • Ulrich Renz

My Most Beautiful Dream

Mein allerschönster Traum

Translation:

Sefâ Jesse Konuk Agnew (English)

Audiobook and video:

www.sefa-bilingual.com/bonus

Password for free access:

English: **BDEN1423**

German: **BDDE1314**

My Most Beautiful Dream

Mein allerschönster Traum

Cornelia Haas · Ulrich Renz

English · bilingual · German

Lulu can't fall asleep. Everyone else is dreaming already – the shark, the elephant, the little mouse, the dragon, the kangaroo, the knight, the monkey, the pilot. And the lion cub. Even the bear has trouble keeping his eyes open …

Hey bear, will you take me along into your dream?

Lulu kann nicht einschlafen. Alle anderen träumen schon – der Haifisch, der Elefant, die kleine Maus, der Drache, das Känguru, der Ritter, der Affe, der Pilot. Und der Babylöwe. Auch dem Bären fallen schon fast die Augen zu …

Du Bär, nimmst du mich mit in deinen Traum?

And with that, Lulu finds herself in bear dreamland. The bear catches fish in Lake Tagayumi. And Lulu wonders, who could be living up there in the trees?

When the dream is over, Lulu wants to go on another adventure. Come along, let's visit the shark! What could he be dreaming?

Und schon ist Lulu im Bären-Traumland. Der Bär fängt Fische im Tagayumi See. Und Lulu wundert sich, wer wohl da oben in den Bäumen wohnt?
Als der Traum zu Ende ist, will Lulu noch mehr erleben. Komm mit, wir besuchen den Haifisch! Was der wohl träumt?

The shark plays tag with the fish. Finally he's got some friends! Nobody's afraid of his sharp teeth.

When the dream is over, Lulu wants to go on another adventure. Come along, let's visit the elephant! What could he be dreaming?

Der Haifisch spielt Fangen mit den Fischen. Endlich hat er Freunde! Keiner hat Angst vor seinen spitzen Zähnen.
Als der Traum zu Ende ist, will Lulu noch mehr erleben. Kommt mit, wir besuchen den Elefanten! Was der wohl träumt?

The elephant is as light as a feather and can fly! He's about to land on the celestial meadow.

When the dream is over, Lulu wants to go on another adventure. Come along, let's visit the little mouse! What could she be dreaming?

Der Elefant ist so leicht wie eine Feder und kann fliegen! Gleich landet er auf der Himmelswiese.
Als der Traum zu Ende ist, will Lulu noch mehr erleben. Kommt mit, wir besuchen die kleine Maus! Was die wohl träumt?

The little mouse watches the fair. She likes the roller coaster best. When the dream is over, Lulu wants to go on another adventure. Come along, let's visit the dragon! What could she be dreaming?

Die kleine Maus schaut sich den Rummel an. Am besten gefällt ihr die Achterbahn.
Als der Traum zu Ende ist, will Lulu noch mehr erleben. Kommt mit, wir besuchen den Drachen! Was der wohl träumt?

The dragon is thirsty from spitting fire. She'd like to drink up the whole lemonade lake.

When the dream is over, Lulu wants to go on another adventure. Come along, let's visit the kangaroo! What could she be dreaming?

Der Drache hat Durst vom Feuerspucken. Am liebsten will er den ganzen Limonadensee austrinken.
Als der Traum zu Ende ist, will Lulu noch mehr erleben. Kommt mit, wir besuchen das Känguru! Was das wohl träumt?

The kangaroo jumps around the candy factory and fills her pouch. Even more of the blue sweets! And more lollipops! And chocolate!
When the dream is over, Lulu wants to go on another adventure. Come along, let's visit the knight! What could he be dreaming?

Das Känguru hüpft durch die Süßigkeitenfabrik und stopft sich den Beutel voll. Noch mehr von den blauen Bonbons! Und mehr Lollis! Und Schokolade!

Als der Traum zu Ende ist, will Lulu noch mehr erleben. Kommt mit, wir besuchen den Ritter! Was der wohl träumt?

The knight is having a cake fight with his dream princess. Oops! The whipped cream cake has gone the wrong way!
When the dream is over, Lulu wants to go on another adventure. Come along, let's visit the monkey! What could he be dreaming?

Der Ritter macht eine Tortenschlacht mit seiner Traumprinzessin. Oh! Die Sahnetorte geht daneben!
Als der Traum zu Ende ist, will Lulu noch mehr erleben. Kommt mit, wir besuchen den Affen! Was der wohl träumt?

Snow has finally fallen in Monkeyland. The whole barrel of monkeys is beside itself and getting up to monkey business.
When the dream is over, Lulu wants to go on another adventure. Come along, let's visit the pilot! In which dream could he have landed?

Endlich hat es einmal geschneit im Affenland! Die ganze Affenbande ist aus dem Häuschen und macht Affentheater.
Als der Traum zu Ende ist, will Lulu noch mehr erleben. Kommt mit, wir besuchen den Piloten! In welchem Traum der wohl gelandet ist?

The pilot flies on and on. To the ends of the earth, and even farther, right on up to the stars. No other pilot has ever managed that.
When the dream is over, everybody is very tired and doesn't feel like going on many adventures anymore. But they'd still like to visit the lion cub.
What could she be dreaming?

Der Pilot fliegt und fliegt. Bis ans Ende der Welt und noch weiter bis zu den Sternen. Das hat noch kein anderer Pilot geschafft.
Als der Traum zu Ende ist, sind alle schon sehr müde und wollen nicht mehr so viel erleben. Aber den Babylöwen wollen sie noch besuchen. Was der wohl träumt?

The lion cub is homesick and wants to go back to the warm, cozy bed.
And so do the others.

And thus begins ...

Der Babylöwe hat Heimweh und will zurück ins warme, kuschelige Bett.
Und die anderen auch.

Und da beginnt …

... Lulu's
most beautiful dream.

... Lulus
allerschönster Traum.

Ulrich Renz • Marc Robitzky

The Wild Swans
Die wilden Schwäne

Translation:

Ludwig Blohm, Pete Savill (English)

Audiobook and video:

www.sefa-bilingual.com/bonus

Password for free access:

English: `WSEN1423`

German: `WSDE1314`

Ulrich Renz · Marc Robitzky

The Wild Swans

Die wilden Schwäne

Based on a fairy tale by

Hans Christian Andersen

English · bilingual · German

Once upon a time there were twelve royal children – eleven brothers and one older sister, Elisa. They lived happily in a beautiful castle.

Es waren einmal zwölf Königskinder – elf Brüder und eine große Schwester, Elisa. Sie lebten glücklich in einem wunderschönen Schloss.

One day the mother died, and some time later the king married again. The new wife, however, was an evil witch. She turned the eleven princes into swans and sent them far away to a distant land beyond the large forest.

Eines Tages starb die Mutter, und einige Zeit später heiratete der König erneut. Die neue Frau aber war eine böse Hexe. Sie verzauberte die elf Prinzen in Schwäne und schickte sie weit weg in ein fernes Land jenseits des großen Waldes.

She dressed the girl in rags and smeared an ointment onto her face that turned her so ugly, that even her own father no longer recognized her and chased her out of the castle. Elisa ran into the dark forest.

Dem Mädchen zog sie Lumpen an und schmierte ihm eine hässliche Salbe ins Gesicht, so dass selbst der eigene Vater es nicht mehr erkannte und aus dem Schloss jagte. Elisa rannte in den dunklen Wald hinein.

Now she was all alone, and longed for her missing brothers from the depths of her soul. As the evening came, she made herself a bed of moss under the trees.

Jetzt war sie ganz allein und sehnte sich aus tiefster Seele nach ihren verschwundenen Brüdern. Als es Abend wurde, machte sie sich unter den Bäumen ein Bett aus Moos.

The next morning she came to a calm lake and was shocked when she saw her reflection in it. But once she had washed, she was the most beautiful princess under the sun.

Am nächsten Morgen kam sie zu einem stillen See und erschrak, als sie darin ihr Spiegelbild sah. Nachdem sie sich aber gewaschen hatte, war sie das schönste Königskind unter der Sonne.

After many days Elisa reached the great sea. Eleven swan feathers were bobbing on the waves.

Nach vielen Tagen erreichte Elisa das große Meer. Auf den Wellen schaukelten elf Schwanenfedern.

As the sun set, there was a swooshing noise in the air and eleven wild swans landed on the water. Elisa immediately recognized her enchanted brothers. They spoke swan language and because of this she could not understand them.

Als die Sonne unterging, war ein Rauschen in der Luft, und elf wilde Schwäne landeten auf dem Wasser. Elisa erkannte ihre verzauberten Brüder sofort. Weil sie aber die Schwanensprache sprachen, konnte sie sie nicht verstehen.

During the day the swans flew away, and at night the siblings snuggled up together in a cave.

One night Elisa had a strange dream: Her mother told her how she could release her brothers from the spell. She should knit shirts from stinging nettles and throw one over each of the swans. Until then, however, she was not allowed to speak a word, or else her brothers would die.
Elisa set to work immediately. Although her hands were burning as if they were on fire, she carried on knitting tirelessly.

Tagsüber flogen die Schwäne fort, nachts kuschelten sich die Geschwister in einer Höhle aneinander.

Eines Nachts hatte Elisa einen sonderbaren Traum: Ihre Mutter sagte ihr, wie sie die Brüder erlösen könne. Aus Brennnesseln solle sie für jeden Schwan ein Hemdchen stricken und es ihm überwerfen. Bis dahin aber dürfe sie kein einziges Wort reden, sonst müssten ihre Brüder sterben.
Elisa machte sich sofort an die Arbeit. Obwohl ihre Hände wie Feuer brannten, strickte sie unermüdlich.

One day hunting horns sounded in the distance. A prince came riding along with his entourage and he soon stood in front of her. As they looked into each other's eyes, they fell in love.

Eines Tages ertönten in der Ferne Jagdhörner. Ein Prinz kam mit seinem Gefolge angeritten und stand schon bald vor ihr. Als die beiden sich in die Augen schauten, verliebten sie sich ineinander.

The prince lifted Elisa onto his horse and rode to his castle with her.

Der Prinz hob Elisa auf sein Pferd und nahm sie mit auf sein Schloss.

The mighty treasurer was anything but pleased with the arrival of the silent beauty. His own daughter was meant to become the prince's bride.

Der mächtige Schatzmeister war über die Ankunft der stummen Schönen alles andere als erfreut. Seine eigene Tochter sollte die Braut des Prinzen werden.

Elisa had not forgotten her brothers. Every evening she continued working on the shirts. One night she went out to the cemetery to gather fresh nettles. While doing so she was secretly watched by the treasurer.

Elisa hatte ihre Brüder nicht vergessen. Jeden Abend arbeitete sie weiter an den Hemdchen. Eines Nachts ging sie hinaus auf den Friedhof, um frische Brennnesseln zu holen. Dabei beobachtete der Schatzmeister sie heimlich.

As soon as the prince was away on a hunting trip, the treasurer had Elisa thrown into the dungeon. He claimed that she was a witch who met with other witches at night.

Sobald der Prinz auf einem Jagdausflug war, ließ der Schatzmeister Elisa in den Kerker werfen. Er behauptete, dass sie eine Hexe sei, die sich nachts mit anderen Hexen treffe.

At dawn, Elisa was fetched by the guards. She was going to be burned to death at the marketplace.

Im Morgengrauen wurde Elisa von den Wachen abgeholt. Sie sollte auf dem Marktplatz verbrannt werden.

No sooner had she arrived there, when suddenly eleven white swans came flying towards her. Elisa quickly threw a shirt over each of them. Shortly thereafter all her brothers stood before her in human form. Only the smallest, whose shirt had not been quite finished, still had a wing in place of one arm.

Kaum war sie dort angekommen, als plötzlich elf weiße Schwäne geflogen kamen. Schnell warf Elisa jedem ein Nesselhemdchen über. Bald standen alle ihre Brüder in Menschengestalt vor ihr. Nur der Kleinste, dessen Hemd nicht ganz fertig geworden war, behielt anstelle eines Armes einen Flügel.

The siblings' joyous hugging and kissing hadn't yet finished as the prince returned. At last Elisa could explain everything to him. The prince had the evil treasurer thrown into the dungeon. And after that the wedding was celebrated for seven days.

And they all lived happily ever after.

Das Herzen und Küssen der Geschwister hatte noch kein Ende genommen, als der Prinz zurückkam. Endlich konnte Elisa ihm alles erklären. Der Prinz ließ den bösen Schatzmeister in den Kerker werfen. Und dann wurde sieben Tage lang Hochzeit gefeiert.

Und wenn sie nicht gestorben sind, dann leben sie noch heute.

Hans Christian Andersen

Hans Christian Andersen was born in the Danish city of Odense in 1805, and died in 1875 in Copenhagen. He gained world fame with his literary fairy-tales such as „The Little Mermaid", „The Emperor's New Clothes" and „The Ugly Duckling". The tale at hand, „The Wild Swans", was first published in 1838. It has been translated into more than one hundred languages and adapted for a wide range of media including theater, film and musical.

Barbara Brinkmann was born in Munich in 1969 and grew up in the foothills of the Bavarian Alps. She studied architecture in Munich and is currently a research associate in the Department of Architecture at the Technical University of Munich. She also works as a freelance graphic designer, illustrator, and author.

Cornelia Haas has been illustrating childrens' and adolescents' books since 2001. She was born near Augsburg, Germany, in 1972. She studied design at the Münster University of Applied Sciences and is currently a professor on the faculty of Münster University of Applied Sciences teaching illustration.

Marc Robitzky, born in 1973, studied at the Technical School of Art in Hamburg and the Academy of Visual Arts in Frankfurt. He works as a freelance illustrator and communication designer in Aschaffenburg (Germany).

Ulrich Renz was born in Stuttgart, Germany, in 1960. After studying French literature in Paris he graduated from medical school in Lübeck and worked as head of a scientific publishing company. He is now a writer of non-fiction books as well as children's fiction books.

Do you like drawing?

Here are the pictures from the story to color in:

www.sefa-bilingual.com/coloring

www.ingramcontent.com/pod-product-compliance
Lightning Source LLC
LaVergne TN
LVHW070447080526
838202LV00035B/2766